JAN 2 6 2017

EARTHQUAKE

by Joyce Markovics

Consultant:
Daphne Thompson, Meteorologist
Educational Outreach Coordinator
Cooperative Institute for Mesoscale Meteorological Studies
National Weather Center

BEARPORT
PUBLISHING

New York, New York

Credits
Cover, © iStockphoto/Thinkstock; 4–5, © Filippo Monteforte/AFP/Getty Images; 6–7, © Tim Clayton/Corbis; 8–9, © STR/AFP/Getty Images; 10–11, © KYODO/Reuters/Corbis; 12–13, © U.S. Navy/Getty Images; 14–15, © Prometheus72/Shutterstock; 15, © AFP/Getty Images; 16–17, © Giorgio Cosulich/Getty Images; 18–19, © Yoshikazu Tsuno/AFP/Getty Images; 20–21, © Joseph Johnson/Getty Images; 22, © Prometheus72/Shutterstock; 23TL, © Tim Ackroyd/Shutterstock; 23TR, © iStockphoto/Thinkstock; 23BR, © AFP/Getty Images.

Publisher: Kenn Goin
Senior Editor: Joyce Tavolacci
Creative Director: Spencer Brinker
Design: Debrah Kaiser
Photo Researcher: Picture Perfect Professionals, LLC

Library of Congress Cataloging-in-Publication Data

Markovics, Joyce L., author.
  Earthquake / by Joyce Markovics.
     pages cm. — (It's a disaster!)
  Audience: Ages 5 to 8.
  Includes bibliographical references and index.
  ISBN 978-1-62724-128-1 (library binding) — ISBN 1-62724-128-0 (library binding)
  1. Earthquakes—Juvenile literature. I. Title.
  QE521.3.M333 2014
  551.22—dc23
                                      2013032756

For more information, write to Bearport Publishing Company, Inc., 45 West 21st Street, Suite 3B, New York, New York 10010. Printed in the United States of America.

10 9 8 7 6 5 4 3 2 1

CONTENTS

EARTHQUAKES

The ground rumbles and shakes.

Sidewalks crack.

An **earthquake** is starting!

Earthquakes can cause large cracks in the ground.

Houses rock back and forth.

Crash!

Buildings fall down.

About one million earthquakes happen each year.

What causes earthquakes?

Deep underground, huge pieces of rock move.

They push and slide against each other.

Then the ground shakes and cracks.

Under the ground, large pieces of rock cover Earth.

9

Most earthquakes are weak.

People cannot feel them.

However, some are very strong.

Strong earthquakes can cause lots of **damage**. They can make bridges and roads fall apart.

11

Big earthquakes can destroy whole towns.

People can get trapped inside buildings.

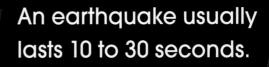

An earthquake usually lasts 10 to 30 seconds.

After an earthquake,
workers look for **survivors**.

Rescuers dig out the
people they find.

Workers take hurt
people to hospitals.

How do you stay safe during an earthquake?

Make sure you do not get hit by falling **debris**.

Debris includes broken glass and pieces of walls.

If the ground shakes, drop to the floor.

Hide under a table or desk to protect your body.

Hold on tight to stay safe.

In some schools, kids practice staying safe in case of an earthquake.

If you are outside, go to an open area.

Stay away from buildings and trees.

Stay out in the open until the shaking stops.

Streetlights and trees can fall during an earthquake.

EARTHQUAKE FACTS

- Alaska has more earthquakes than any other state.

- Florida and North Dakota have the fewest earthquakes.

- Earthquakes can cause mudslides, fires, floods, and huge waves called tsunamis.

- Earthquakes called moonquakes sometimes occur on the moon.

GLOSSARY

damage (DAM-ij) harm or ruin

debris (duh-BREE) pieces of buildings or other objects that have been destroyed

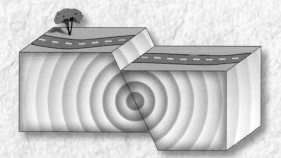

earthquake (URTH-kwayk) a shaking of the ground caused by the sudden movement of rocks below Earth's surface

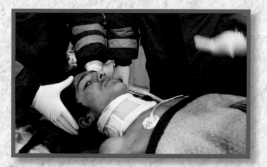

survivors (sur-VYE-vurz) people who live through a disaster or horrible event

INDEX

READ MORE

Riley, Joelle. *Earthquakes (Pull Ahead Books: Forces of Nature).* Minneapolis, MN: Lerner (2008).

Walker, Sally M. *Earthquakes (Early Bird Earth Science).* Minneapolis, MN: Lerner (2007).

LEARN MORE ONLINE

To learn more about earthquakes, visit
www.bearportpublishing.com/ItsaDisaster!

ABOUT THE AUTHOR

Joyce Markovics lives along the Hudson River in Tarrytown, New York. She felt the Earth tremble during the 2011 Virginia earthquake.